INTERNET
ANIMAL
STARS

SLOTH POWER

REBECCA FELIX

Lerner Publications ◆ Minneapolis

Lerner Publications Company
An imprint of Lerner Publishing Group, Inc.
241 First Avenue North
Minneapolis, MN 55401 USA

For reading levels and more information, look up this title at www.lernerbooks.com.
Main body text set in Caecilia Com
Typeface provided by Monotype

Library of Congress Cataloging-in-Publication Data

Names: Felix, Rebecca, 1984– author.
Title: Sloth power / Rebecca Felix.
Description: Minneapolis : Lerner Publications, [2021] | Series: Internet animal stars | Includes bibliographical references and index. | Audience: Ages 6–10 | Audience: Grades 2–3 | Summary: "What animal likes to hang out on the internet? The sloth! This guide draws in young readers with an appealing social-media-inspired design while delivering curriculum content, such as the life cycle, habitat, and diet"-- Provided by publisher.
Identifiers: LCCN 2019058478 (print) | LCCN 2019058479 (ebook) | ISBN 9781541597129 (library binding) | ISBN 9781728402925 (paperback) | ISBN 9781728400402 (ebook)
Subjects: LCSH: Sloths--Juvenile literature.
Classification: LCC QL737.E2 F45 2021 (print) | LCC QL737.E2 (ebook) | DDC 599.3/13--dc23

LC record available at https://lccn.loc.gov/2019058468
LC ebook record available at https://lccn.loc.gov/2019058469

Manufactured in the United States of America
1 – CG – 7/15/20

#SlothSquad

PAGE PLUS!

Scan QR codes throughout the book for videos of cute animals!

Introduction

SLOTH POWER

What do you know about sloths? These **mellow** mammals move slowly. They are called the slowest animals on Earth! Humans love sloths. The internet has tons of charming sloth **content**.

#FamilyTree
Sloths are related to armadillos and anteaters.

Learn about these gentle animals. Then discover how sloths became internet stars!

#SuperSloth

Chapter 1

SLOTH LIFE

★ Bitty Babies ★

Sloth babies cling to their mothers after birth. They don't let go for up to six months!

The babies **nurse** for about one month. Baby sloths let go of their mothers when they can feed themselves.

Sloth mothers give their babies bits of food.

#BabySloth

★ Adult Species ★

Young sloths stay with their mothers for two to four years, depending on the species.

There are six sloth species. All sloths have long arms and long claws.

The largest species weighs around 17 pounds (8 kg).

Scan this QR code to see a sleepy sloth!

#GoodBoy

★ Senior ★ Sloths

Sloths spend most of their lives alone and in trees. They live up to thirty years in the wild.

Sloth **predators** include hawks, eagles, and jaguars.

Sloths visit the ground once a week to poop. Many are killed by predators during these trips.

Chapter 2

FORESTS, FOOD & FUR

Sloths live in the forests of Central America and South America.

Some sloths live in several trees during their lifetimes. Others live their entire lives in the same tree!

Sloths spend their days sleeping and eating. They sleep between ten to twenty hours a day.

Sloths eat fruit, leaves, **buds**, insects, and small lizards.

Sloths also eat a type of **algae** that grows only on their fur. There is also a species of moth that lives only in sloth fur!

#DungEggs
Sloth moths lay their eggs in sloth poop!

Sloths eat and **digest** slowly. It can take them one month to digest a single meal.

Scan this QR code to see a sloth eating a leaf!

Sloths climb and crawl slowly too. But they're fast swimmers! Swimming and sleeping sloths amaze people.

So do shy sloths, playful sloths, and silly sloths!

Chapter 3

SLOTHS IN POP CULTURE

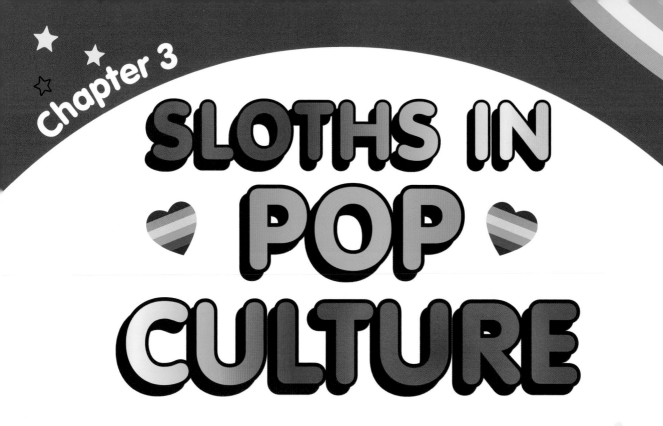

Sloths are social media superstars! But how and why did these drowsy tree-dwellers become famous?

Researchers think it started with a 2010 video called "Meet the Sloths." The video shows baby sloths at a sloth **orphanage** in Costa Rica. The video went **viral**. Soon, sloths did too.

Hi there!

Experts also think sloths are popular because of the animal's behavior. People admire sloths for living quiet, relaxed lives. Many humans want to live like this!

Lots of people just think sloths are cute. Some sloths have become famous around the world.

#SlothSmile

★ Standout Sloths ★

Online sloth stars become famous for many reasons. Some star in a single meme. Others are featured on zoo social media accounts!

Superstar! EDWARD THE SLOTH

Like Edward, this baby sloth loves its stuffed toy.

Edward was born at the London Zoo in 2015. Zoo staff posted a video of him clinging to a teddy bear. Edward's mom couldn't raise him. The toy was her **surrogate**! The video went viral. People loved the itty-bitty baby sloth.

MEME BREAK!

TRYING YOGA FOR THE FIRST TIME LIKE

ME WHEN IT'S MY TURN TO DO PULL-UPS IN FRONT OF THE WHOLE GYM CLASS

BEGGING DAD TO BUY THAT TREAT, PLEEEEEEEEEASE

TEACHER: YOU'LL NEED A PARTNER FOR THIS PROJECT
ME LOOKING AT MY FRIEND:

MEME BREAK!

WHEN MY OLDER BROTHER GETS HOME AND I'M WAITING FOR HIM TO FIND OUT I BROKE HIS HOVERBOARD

SLOTHS ROCK!

Sloth stardom may be here to stay! Sloth content has remained popular for years.

Sloths have spread offline too. The animals appear on clothing, school supplies, and more.

Sloths even have a holiday! International Sloth Day is October 20. It raises awareness about protecting sloths.

#SlothStar

algae: a simple plant with no leaves or stems that usually grows near water

bud: a small part of a plant that will grow into a new flower, leaf, or shoot

content: ideas, facts, and images available online

digest: to break down food in the body

mellow: calm and relaxed

nurse: to drink milk from a mother's body

orphanage: a place that cares for people or animals who have lost their parents

predator: an animal that eats other animals to survive

surrogate: a thing or person that takes the place of something else

viral: spreading quickly to many people over the internet